CORNISH CHINA CLAY TRAINS IN COLOUR

Maurice Dart

Ian Allan PUBLISHING

Front cover: Two locos for the price of one: No 37672 is reflected in the water as it passes Golant with loaded clay hoods bound for Fowey on 22 July 1987. *Maurice Dart*

Back cover: On the bright morning of 23 July 1999 No 66123 takes a rake of loaded CDA wagons from Lostwithiel down the branch to Fowey with passing pedestrians oblivious to the superb new type of locomotive passing, whilst small boats sit peacefully on the river awaiting their weekend sailors. *Maurice Dart*

Title page: A shunter is checking the train of loaded CDA wagons which are standing in Wheal Henry loop headed by No 37668 carrying Petroleum Sector decals, which is waiting to set off with its load to Fowey 18 April 1995. The stack of Wheal Henry pan kiln has been reduced in height. *Maurice Dart*

First published 2000

ISBN 0 7110 2753 6

Published by Ian Allan Publishing

an imprint of Ian Allan Publishing Ltd, Terminal House, Shepperton, Surrey TW17 8AS.

Printed by Ian Allan Printing Ltd, Riverdene Business Park, Hersham, Surrey KT12 4RG.

Code: 0006/B1

Introduction

The china clay industry can trace its origins to China, where since AD700 the mineral called kaolin, which is a hydrated aluminium silicate ($Al_2O_3 2SiO_2 2H_2O$), has been used as an ingredient in the manufacture of pottery. This mineral has been formed over many centuries by feldspar crystals in granite being subjected to high temperatures in moist conditions in the ground which cause it to decompose, forming a white powder which is a kaolinised granite. Evidence shows that small china clay workings were in existence north of St Austell on Hensbarrow Downs from around 1584 but the main growth stemmed from 1745/6 when the mineral was discovered at Tregonning Hill in west Cornwall and then in far greater quantities around Carloggas, northwest of St Austell. The entrepreneur William Cookworthy, a chemist from Kingsbridge in south Devon, obtained some samples of china clay, set up a wholesale chemical business in Plymouth and made visits to Cornwall to prospect for the mineral. In 1768 he patented the manufacture of porcelain and moved to Bristol where he owned a factory which was eventually taken over by a consortium of potters from Staffordshire, prominent among them being Josiah Wedgwood. During the 19th century small clay workings were established around Cornwall by local entrepreneurs and a gradual expansion of the industry occurred.

At first the clay was separated from the water used to extract it (known as 'washing out the clay and settling it out') and the thickened slurry was made into piles and allowed to dry off slowly in the open air (know as 'air drying'). This was a very slow process and from 1845 coal-fired 'pan kilns' were gradually introduced which greatly speeded up the process by spreading out the clay on tiles which formed the pan of the kiln beneath which passed the hot gases formed by the combustion of coal in furnaces.

Left: On 23 September 1960, '42xx' 2-8-0T No 4273 is seen at Fowey with a train of empties for St Blazey. Fowey was served by lines running from Lostwithiel with services for workmen succumbing on 31 December 1934. The line to Lostwithiel lost its passenger services on 4 January 1965. The line beyond Fowey to St Blazey was converted into a road for use by EEC after closure in 1968, but the line remains open for traffic between Fowey and Lostwithiel. *R.C. Riley*

When dried, the clay was shovelled off the pan and placed in the storage area known as the 'linhay' which was usually at a lower level. In order to transport the clay to other areas of the country, harbours were built at West Polmear in the 1790s by Charles Rashleigh, later renamed Charlestown, at Pentewan in the 1820s and at Par in the 1830s. To transport the clay to these harbours it was necessary to haul it in wagons pulled by teams of horses along twisting, narrow roads which became deeply rutted, the terrain necessitating the negotiation of numerous long steep hills with assisting and relief horses required en route. This was very slow and cumbersome so in June 1829 the port of Pentewan was linked to St Austell by a horse-worked tramway of 2ft 6in gauge which from 1873 became worked by steam traction.

In 1841 Squire Thomas Treffry started the building of a standard gauge tramway to link clay works on Hendra Downs near St Dennis with the harbour at Newquay, which opened by 1849. He followed this in 1842 with another standard gauge line from the clay works at Moliniss, near Bugle, to Pontsmill, where it linked up with a canal which ran to Par Harbour. Later, in 1855, this line was extended to Par Harbour to save transhipment to the canal at Pontsmill. Next on the scene came the Newquay & Cornwall Junction Railway which, in 1869, opened a broad gauge line from Burngullow on the Cornwall Railway to Drinnick Mill via Carpella.

The biggest development came on 21 July 1873 when the Cornwall Minerals Railway (CMR) was incorporated. The railway purchased the two Treffry Tramways and rebuilt them to be suitable for locomotive working, which entailed some route diversions, and took over the line to Drinnick Mill which had been worked by a contractor called William West from St Blazey. The CMR also built new lines linking Drinnick Mill with the St Dennis area, as well as lines between Bugle and Newquay and down the Fal valley to Retew and Melangoose Mill. It built its locomotive works and running shed at St Blazey, together with a wagon works at the site. Already by 1870 a network of lines encircled the clay-producing area around St Austell which greatly assisted the movement of the mineral from the clay works to the harbours, and the line from St Blazey to Fowey via Pinnock Tunnel was opened by the CMR on 1 June 1874. Movement was further assisted when the line from Lostwithiel to Fowey reopened in 1895.

However, from 1 October 1877 all of the CMR lines were worked by the Great Western Railway and despite the CMR amalgamating with the GWR on 1 July 1889, 'break of gauge' existed at Par and at Drinnick Mill with transhipment facilities until 23 May 1892. Further developments took place in due course when the CMR opened the Goonbarrow branch from Goonbarrow Junction, south of Bugle to clay works at Gunheath and Carbean

3

4

on 2 October 1893, which the parent company worked until the GWR took over in 1896. Next, on 1 July 1912, the GWR opened an extension line from Melangoose Mill to Meledor Mill, with, much later, a line from Trenance Junction, west of St Austell, to Bojea sidings opening on 1 May 1920, and an extension to Lansalson opening on the 24th of the same month. This completed the china clay mineral line network around St Austell. During this period pan kilns grew in size and clay was transported as blocks, in powder form in bags after milling, as loose small lumps or in casks made of wood and also as lumps bagged up.

The first line closure took place in 1918 when the Pentewan Railway closed. On the other lines traffic built up, with china clay being carried in open wagons covered with sheets and in box vans. During the interwar years several of the clay companies amalgamated, one of the groups being English China Clays (ECCI) which became the leading clay producer in the world.

After World War 2 mechanical drying methods were gradually introduced and this led to the closure of many of the older pan kilns, which in turn led to the closure of some of the clay branch lines which served them. The closures were Parkandillick to St Dennis Junction on 6 February 1966, St Blazey to Fowey via Pinnock Tunnel on 1 July 1968 (after which it was converted into a 'haul road' for lorries), the industrial branch from Par Harbour to Par Moor kilns during 1977, the Trenance valley in two stages in 1964 and 1968, the Goonbarrow branch in stages during 1965 and 1968, the Wheal Rose branch (which was worked as a siding from Bugle) in 1964, the Retew branch to Melador Mill on 3 April 1982 and the Carbis branch on 31 December 1989. The lines to Moorswater and to Pontsmill lost their clay traffic when the kilns they served closed but both still remained operational. The ex-Bodmin & Wadebridge Railway (later London & South Western Railway) line from Boscarne Junction to Wenford kilns closed on 21 November 1983, the section on to Wenford Bridge having closed on 13 February 1967.

During the postwar period the famous clay hood wagons were introduced, replacing open wagons, and more recently various forms of large-capacity covered vans such as Continental Rail wagons, Tiger wagons and Polybulk wagons have been brought in. Another development was the introduction of processes for producing the finished clay as a high-density slurry and to transport this several types of tank wagons were introduced. During 1988 the clay hood wagons were replaced by CDA hopper wagons, with CEA wagons following in 1999.

So, today we are left with the line from Burngullow Junction which serves Burngullow Tube Press, with Crugwallins siding (450,000 tonnes per annum) (shortly to be augmented with the new Millennium siding), Kernick and Treviscoe Dryers (approximately 130,000 tonnes per annum), Parkandillick Buell and Calciner (approximately 120,000 tonnes per annum) and Blackpool slurry plant near Burngullow which sends out approximately 200,000 tonnes per annum, mainly to Caledonian Paper Mills at Irvine. At Goonbarrow Junction is the Rocks Dryers complex, with approximately 450,000 tonnes per annum being sent by rail. The complex at Par sends out 20,000 tonnes per annum which is mainly milled clay in bags from the European Milling Centre, whilst across the River Tamar in Devon is Marsh Mills Dryers served by a sharply curved and steeply graded line from Tavistock Junction yard from which approximately 270,000 tonnes per annum are sent out by rail. During 1998 an overall figure of 1.3 million tonnes of clay were moved by rail, some of this being ball clay.

During 1999 ECCI became part of the French company Imatel which has now changed its name to Imerys and currently employs 2,700 people in Cornwall and 300 at Lee Moor and Marsh Mills. Around 60 grades of clay are produced and exported to over 100 countries, of which an average of 30,000 tonnes per week go out from Fowey. Approximately 88% of the production is exported, which earns £220 million, of which £125 million goes into the local economy.

This collection of photographs attempts to portray a general picture of the locomotives and trains which have worked and are working clay traffic, including those using some of the high-capacity CDA wagons which from February 1988 could carry 32 tonnes compared with the 12 tonnes carried by the clay hoods, along with a variety of vans and slurry tanks. The network has shrunk but the traffic over the past 10 or so years has remained buoyant. Since 1988 the clay industry has acquired its own fleet of shunting locos in Cornwall and these are illustrated together with a few scenes at non-ECCI/Imerys-owned locations.

Left: Again seen on 23 September 1960,. 0-6-0PT No 9655 passes through Lostwithiel. Notice the station name-board advertising the branch line service to Fowey and the palm trees and flower beds on the down platform. *R. C. Riley*

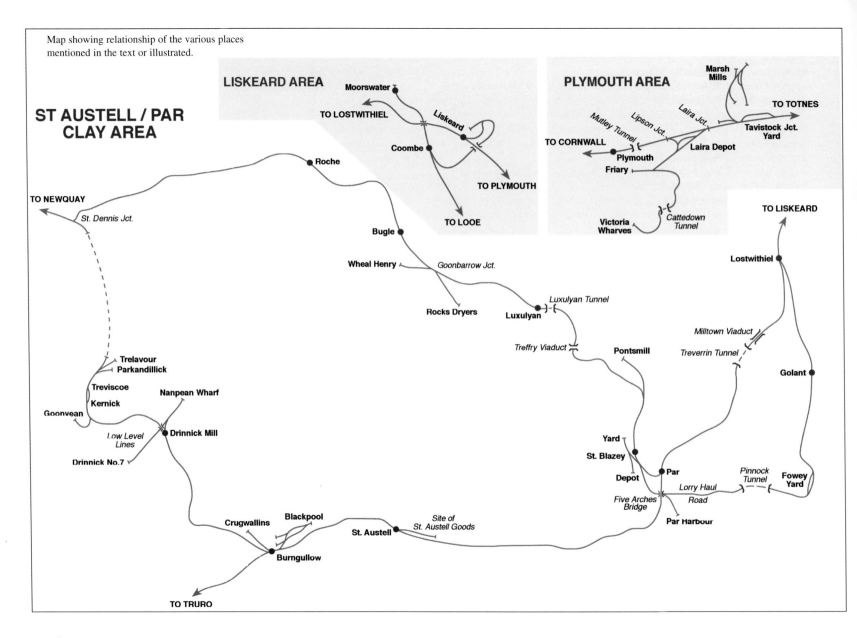

Map showing relationship of the various places mentioned in the text or illustrated.

ST AUSTELL / PAR CLAY AREA

LISKEARD AREA

Moorswater

TO LOSTWITHIEL

Liskeard

Coombe

TO PLYMOUTH

TO LOOE

PLYMOUTH AREA

Marsh Mills

TO TOTNES

Mutley Tunnel

Lipson Jct.

Laira Jct.

Tavistock Jct. Yard

TO CORNWALL

Plymouth Friary

Laira Depot

Victoria Wharves

Cattedown Tunnel

Roche

TO NEWQUAY

St. Dennis Jct.

Bugle

Wheal Henry

Goonbarrow Jct.

Rocks Dryers

Luxulyan

Luxulyan Tunnel

Treffry Viaduct

Pontsmill

Trelavour
Parkandillick

Treviscoe

Kernick

Goonvean

Nanpean Wharf

Low Level Lines

Drinnick Mill

Drinnick No.7

Yard

St. Blazey

Depot

Par

TO LISKEARD

Lostwithiel

Milltown Viaduct

Treverrin Tunnel

Golant

Pinnock Tunnel

Fowey Yard

Five Arches Bridge

Lorry Haul Road

Par Harbour

Crugwallins

Blackpool

St. Austell

Site of St. Austell Goods

Burngullow

TO TRURO

6

The locomotive depot at St Blazey maintains the fleet of clay locos for English, Welsh and Scottish Railways (EWS) and also the various wagons and vans used for its transportation, all of the work being carried out in the original Cornwall Minerals Railway wagon works building, now modernised. Outside is the turntable which is still used at times to turn Class 08 locos, and others, to ease flange wear or for duty at Fowey where the loco is required to face in the opposite direction from that normally used at St Blazey. Opposite, the semi-roundhouse loco shed still stands, with rails leading into it, albeit no longer accessible from the turntable.

Acknowledgements

I would like to thank Ivor Bowditch, Public Relations Manager of ECCI (now Imerys), for continuing permission to access the various sidings, and to the captains and managers at the locations for their help and co-operation. Thanks must also be extended to Huw Phillips, who was EWS Manager for Devon and Cornwall based at St Blazey, for his co-operation about movements, and also to the depot staff, past and present, at St Blazey for their ready assistance with information, amongst whom Adrian Cannon and George Hemmett deserve special mention. Included with the staff at St Blazey are, of course, the loco crews, guards and shunters.

My special thanks to Mr R. C. Riley for supplying some slides of the steam era for this book and also to John A. M. Vaughan and George Hemmett for additional photographic material.

Mention must also be made of several willing friends who have acted as chauffeur to me on various jaunts around the area, amongst whom are John A. M. Vaughan, Gary Hibbs, the late Tom Corin, Pat Dennison, Jill Green and Renée Barrett, without whose help it would have been most awkward and time-consuming to reach some of these locations. One other who deserves mention for assistance with information on movements and with chauffeuring is Steve Lightfoot.

My thanks are extended to Gillian Searle of the Bodmin & Wenford Railway for her able assistance in preparing the text and photo captions for submission to the publishers. I must also thank Brian Rose of Ian Allan for badgering me during his visits to Bodmin General station with the idea of this book. My thanks also go out to anyone who by lapse of thought may have been omitted from this list.

Lastly, I must thank the late Emily Hancock for again permitting me to transform one of her rooms into a study to put this book together.

Maurice Dart
St Austell
March 2000

Reference Sources

Industrial Locomotives, Handbook EL10, Industrial Railway Society
Track Layout Diagrams of the GWR and BRWR (Sections for East Cornwall and South Devon), R. A. Cooke
An Illustrated History of West Country China Clay Trains, John Vaughan, Oxford Publishing Co
The Newquay Line and Its Branches, John Vaughan, Oxford Publishing Co
Also my own extensive collection of notes and maps acquired over many years.

Visits to China Clay Sidings

These can usually be arranged by application to Mr I. Bowditch, Public Relations Manager, Imerys, John Keay House, St Austell, Cornwall PL25 4DJ or by writing to the author at 20 Bodmin Road, St Austell, Cornwall PL25 5AE. I am prepared to act as guide for visits but must point out that private transport is a necessity.

Dedication

This book is dedicated to the staff, train crews and shunters at St Blazey depot.

Passing beneath the viaduct carrying the West of England main line to the west of Liskeard, No 37673 and its rake of CDAs form a Moorswater to Carne Point service on 14 June 1989. *John Vaughan*

Left: Although relatively new at this date — 20 July 1960 — the Western Region's diesel-hydraulics saw use on freight services in Cornwall — a pattern that was to exist until the final withdrawal of the types in the 1970s. Here 'Warship' No D816 *Eclipse* is nearing Par Sands on a train of empty wagons from Fowey. *R. C. Riley*

Above: A number of mineral lines were constructed to capitalise on the potential wealth to be generated from the exploitation of china clay. One of these was the Lee Moor Tramway. This line — built to the Dartmoor gauge of 4ft 6in – originally opened in September 1854 and closed one month later following an accident on one of the inclines. It was reopened in 1858 and was to survive until 1939. Partly reopened for two years after World War 2, the line fell into disuse and the route was finally lifted in 1961/62. Pictured at the Wheal Martyn museum, near St Austell on 26 August 1981 is *Lee Moor No 1*, a 4ft 6in gauge Peckett 0-4-0ST (Works No 783) of 1899. *R. C. Riley*

Above: On 9 August 1967 0-4-0 fireless loco Bagnall No 3121, built in 1957, stands adjacent to the point where it was recharged with steam from the power station at English China Clays' drying plant at Marsh Mills, with the steampipe connected to its reservoir. The loco is standing at the top end of the line into the complex. The lefthand line behind the loco leads to the stabling siding, whilst that on the right leads to the works area. The main branch climbs up at a gradient of approximately 1 in 40 to 1 in 50 to reach this point; following closure of the ex-GWR line to Tavistock the approach was realigned from a date quoted variously as 4 April or 27 June 1965 to lead from the east at Tavistock Junction yard. This loco is preserved awaiting restoration on the Bodmin & Wenford Railway and is at present stored at the back end of the sidings at Bodmin Parkway yard. *Maurice Dart*

Above: The replacement for the fireless loco at Marsh Mills was this 0-4-0 diesel-hydraulic built by English Electric Vehicles in 1970. Works No 3987 is seen standing on the stabling siding on 25 September 1988 awaiting a move to Cornwall to work at Moorswater Dryer. *Maurice Dart*

Above: The successor to the English electric loco at Marsh Mills was ex-BR Class 08 loco No 08398, which was transferred from Fowey yard, but when the shunting at ECCI Marsh Mills was eventually taken over by British Rail No 08398 was transferred back to Cornwall to Blackpool sidings. On 23 July 1997 Class 09 No 09008, allocated to St Blazey, slowly eases CDA clay hopper wagons into position for loading in one of the covered loading areas, with the driver watching his train as well as the hand signals being given by the shunter standing beside the entrance to the shed. The loco was actually allocated to Cardiff Canton for maintenance and carries the depot's emblem on a plate below the cab window. *Maurice Dart*

Left: The Burngullow to Irvine train of clay slurry tanks for Caledonian Paper Mills comes off the Royal Albert Bridge and enters Devon on 15 September 1991 hauled by a pair of Class 37 locos. No 37411 is in Railfreight Distribution livery and No 37420 carries InterCity livery and is named *The Scottish Hosteller*; both locos carry the Cornish lizard emblem of St Blazey depot. The tank wagons are easily recognisable as 'silver bullets'. *Maurice Dart*

Right: 0-4-0 Diesel-hydraulic EEV No 3987/1970 was transferred from Marsh Mills to Moorswater, named *Sharon* and numbered P401D. On 29 July 1990 the recently transferred *Sharon* stands at the north end of the sidings at ECCI Moorswater Dryer. Clay ceased to be dried here on 14 December 1996 and the stock was removed by March 1997. The line was then mothballed and used only for Engineering Department trains but in July 1999 a cement plant took occupation of the site and traffic resumed. *Sharon* was transferred to work at ECC Carbonates at Quidhampton near Salisbury. *Maurice Dart*

Left: During 1987 a long train of empty clay hoods hauled by No 37175 and bound for ECCI Moorswater crosses Moorswater viaduct which is 147ft high with a length of 318yd. *John Vaughan*

Above: In May 1975 a visiting railway society enjoyed a trip in a brake van from Boscarne to Wenford kilns and back. The train is at ECCI Wenford in the charge of No 08377 ready for the return trip with the society's headboard mounted on the loco. The Wenford line closed on 21 November 1983, since when clay has been moved from there by road. On the right can be seen some of the disused pan kilns, which were six in number, with their stacks (chimneys). All of these gradually became disused, being replaced by one modern rotary dryer. *John Vaughan*

Above: On a weekend when the down main line through Par station was closed for reballasting, all down freight trains on the Saturday were terminating at Lostwithiel. InterCity-liveried No 37416 bearing the unofficial name 'Mt Fuji' and No 37674 with Railfreight Distribution decals have brought the down air-braked service from Bescot into the down loop east of the station on 9 October 1993. Owing to the length of the train, which consists of Polybulk wagons and Cargowagons, it is being divided into two sections for stabling in the yard adjacent to the station. Several semaphore signals are visible with the sidings which served the disused milk factory on the left. *Maurice Dart*

Right: This up-to-date scene shows No 66120 bringing a train of loaded CDA wagons into Lostwithiel up loop on 23 July 1999 where it will run round the train before taking it onwards to Fowey. *Maurice Dart*

Above: On 23 July 1999 No 66124 brings a rake of empty CDA wagons from Lostwithiel up loop over the crossover on to the down main line to take them to one of the loading points beyond Par, on this occasion probably to Rocks Dryers. *Maurice Dart*

Right: EWS-liveried No 60027 heads a rake of loaded CDA wagons through Lostwithiel station mid-afternoon on 23 July 1999. The loco placed the train in the loop, ran round the train and took it to the yard before heading to St Blazey depot. The down signal is off for a Class 158 sprinter at the down platform. *Maurice Dart*

Above: On 22 July 1987 a long string of empty clay hoods passes Golant, hauled by No 37672. Despite it being a dull cloudy day, the loco is reflected well in the water. *Maurice Dart*

Right: The original traverser at the unloading point at Fowey Jetties on 10 July 1987 with a clay hood, which has just been emptied, passing across to gain the exit line which is seen with its 'Beetle' wagon mover on the lower left of the photo. In the background is visible part of the plant used for discharging clay brought in by lorries for loading into ships. *Maurice Dart*

Left: When the CDA wagons were introduced at Fowey, the unloading system was modernised and given increased capacity by the provision of a second traverser. Work is in progress on this whilst wagons are unloaded on the original one during the afternoon of 19 February 1988. *Maurice Dart*

Above: Mid-afternoon on 19 February 1988 finds No 37674 with its driver posing beside the loco at the head of a rake of the newly introduced CDA wagons in Fowey yard, awaiting the road to Lostwithiel. *Maurice Dart*

Left: On withdrawal of the Blackstone-engined Class 10 diesel shunters by British Rail, somewhat of a surprise occurred when ECC purchased three of them for use at Fowey yard: two as working locos and one as 'spare' to provide parts for the others. On 10 July 1987 they are together at the east end of the yard and from left to right are Nos D3452, D3497 (the spares loco) and D3476, which is coupled to the Fowey shunters' truck. These locos were eventually rendered surplus to requirements when British Rail took over shunting duties in the yard and No D3452, together with some parts from No D3497, was purchased for the Bodmin & Wenford Railway. It is at present employed as station pilot at Bodmin General. No D3497 was cut up at Fowey and No D3476 went to the South Yorkshire Railway Preservation Society at Meadowhall, Sheffield.
Maurice Dart

Right: Since British Rail took over shunting duties at Fowey a variety of different locos from St Blazey have worked there. The wet and murky evening of 22 April 1997 finds No 08576, carrying small numerals, at the entrance to Fowey yard slowly propelling a new 'barrier' wagon, converted from a steel hopper wagon, down into the yard. These barrier wagons, which are locally referred to as 'reach wagons', have now been replaced by a pair of converted fuel tank wagons. These wagons are required in order to provide sufficient clearance between the front of the loco and the back end of the last CDA wagon in a rake for unloading.
Maurice Dart

Left: A train of around 40 loaded clay hood wagons bound for Fowey yard tackles the winding 1 in 80 climb to Treverrin Tunnel from Par on 18 April 1985 in the charge of No 37181, which carries the lizard emblem of the short-lived Cornish Railways, leading No 37247. *John Vaughan*

Above: Railfreight-liveried No 37672 has brought a string of loaded clay hoods from Parkandillick into Par on 1 September 1987 and reversed them into Chapel siding to allow passenger trains a clear run to Lostwithiel, after the passage of which the loco will take the wagons on to Fowey for unloading. *Maurice Dart*

Right: No 08954 waits for the shunters to open the gates at Par Bridge crossing with a mixed rake of loaded wagons from Par Harbour to St Blazey Yard on 17 August 1992. *Maurice Dart*

Above: From 1953 the internal railway system at Par Harbour was worked by a pair of 0-4-0STs built by Bagnall's which had 'cut-down mountings and cabs' to permit passage under a bridge which carried the Western Region (BR) main line west of Par station adjacent to Par Harbour signalbox and sidings. In spring 1962 *Alfred* (Bagnall No 3058/53) moves wagons out from the harbour area towards the transfer sidings. The building in the background to the left of the locomotive is Cornwall Mills which produced ground mineral products. *Alfred* is now preserved on the Bodmin & Wenford Railway. *George Hemmett*

Right: Par Harbour is served by a branch line running from St Blazey which is worked by the St Blazey yard pilot loco. During mid-afternoon on 23 October 1995 No 08786, with two shunters riding on the steps, has just passed below Five Arches bridge and is about to traverse the grass-covered rails at the entrance to Par Harbour, where it will collect loaded wagons to take to St Blazey. *Maurice Dart*

Above: No 08954 is seen earlier the same day (17 August 1992) waiting alongside the Cambrian Bulk Clay Store at Par Harbour with loaded wagons which it will shortly take up the branch to St Blazey yard for marshalling into the late afternoon departure for Bescot. Beyond the train can be seen storage linhays from which clay is loaded into the wagons. *Maurice Dart*

Right: Locomotives are not permitted to traverse the rails beyond the Cambrian Bulk Clay Store around the curve to the New Linhay railside loading bays, so between these points the motive power employed is a clay loader modified to act as a wagon pusher. It is seen on 23 October 1995 propelling a loaded Tiphook Rail Tiger wagon around the curve which crosses two internal harbour roadways towards the exchange sidings. *Maurice Dart*

Above: In May 1989 a blue-liveried Class 08 loco couples up to loaded PRA wagons at ECCI Pontsmill which it will bring out over the connection from the works area and then set the train back on to the brake van to cover the short distance to St Blazey yard. *John Vaughan*

Right: The curve which links Par to St Blazey traverses two underline bridges which cross the canal from Pontsmill to Par Harbour and the Par River. Between these bridges is a foot crossing for pedestrians which is on the route of the original Treffry Tramway but is, of course, somewhat higher at this point. Mid-afternoon on 8 October 1991 finds No 37672 *Freight Transport Association* bringing the train bound for Bescot out of St Blazey yard across the river bridge with one of the gates which protect the foot crossing visible. The loco carries Railfreight Distribution decals and St Blazey depot lizard plates. *Maurice Dart*

Left: The scene at Goonbarrow Junction south of Bugle on the line from Par to Newquay as No 25216 waits for the road out from Wheal Henry siding with a long line of loaded clay hoods from Rocks Dryers bound for Fowey on 5 August 1976. The stack of Wheal Henry pan kiln can be seen on the left. Rocks Dryers is behind the photographer who is standing on the inlet line, and Rosevear siding curves around to the left just below the grassy bank. This was taken before a revised and expanded layout was provided to cater for newly installed mechanical drying units. *Maurice Dart*

Below left: On 5 August 1976 No D1071 *Western Renown* is watched closely by a shunter as it slowly passes over pointwork to exit from the Rocks Dryers complex to reach Goonbarrow Junction after dropping a long string of empty clay hoods. *Maurice Dart*

Right: No 37672 *Freight Transport Association* stands on one of the three storage sidings at Goonbarrow Junction on the afternoon of 17 August 1992, waiting for a set of wagons to be loaded at Rocks Dryers which are out of view to the right of the camera. The loco carries Railfreight Distribution decals and the driver is in the signalbox which, together with the storage sidings, is situated between the line to Newquay and the china clay drying plant. *Maurice Dart*

Above: On 19 August 1999 No 66048 waits at Goonbarrow Junction after dropping off a train of empty CDA wagons at Rocks Dryers. The driver is talking to the shunter who is standing by the loco awaiting instructions for the next movement to be carried out. *Maurice Dart*

Right: On 23 April 1987 a train consisting of three types of wagons loaded with china clay is eased out of the sidings at ECCI Rocks Dryers towards Wheal Henry loop by blue-liveried No 37175 which carries a large BR logo. Goonbarrow Junction signalbox is on the left, beside which there are lines of empty clay hood wagons standing in the three storage sidings. *John Vaughan*

Left: The shortened stack of Wheal Henry pan kiln peeps over the mound on the left as a train of loaded CDA wagons from Rocks Dryers waits in Wheal Henry siding behind No 66048 for the road to St Blazey and onwards to Fowey. This loco had arrived in Cornwall on one of the 'Eclipse' specials on 11 August and had failed, its place on the return working being taken by No 66155. It was taken to St Blazey and repaired and then utilised on clay workings as seen here on 19 August 1999. *Maurice Dart*

Right: During the mid-1980s Rocks Dryers acquired its own loco to position wagons for loading and take them out to Wheal Henry siding for collection by British Rail. When the CDA wagons arrived it was returned to the manufacturer for modification to enable it to work with them and on return, in common with other ECCI locos, it gained a name. The 4w diesel-hydraulic loco built by Rolls-Royce/Sentinel in 1960 (works No 10029), numbered P403D and named *Denise*, waits with two loaded CDA wagons in Wheal Henry siding after having given members of the Branch Line Society an impromptu ride over some of the layout on 29 May 1992. The siding set in concrete no longer connects with the other lines at its extremity. In the distance some BLS members are inspecting the remains of the Goonbarrow branch which climbs past the siding on a gradient of 1 in 39 and is retained as a shunting neck. *Maurice Dart*

Left: When *Denise* was returned to the builders in 1987 for modification to enable it to work with air-braked stock, a replacement loco worked at Rocks Dryers for a few weeks. The unnumbered 0-6-0 diesel-hydraulic built by Rolls-Royce/Sentinel is positioning clay hood wagons for loading on 28 January of that year. *Maurice Dart*

Right: A deserted scene at Rocks Dryers on 21 September 1992 with *Denise* running past the loading area on the reception road for empty wagons, having just passed below the bridge for pedestrians which spans the sidings. *Denise* was later required for use at Crugwallins siding near Burngullow and was replaced by ex-BR No 08398, now numbered P402D and named *Annabel. Maurice Dart*

Above: No 37668 carrying Petroleum Sector decals and the goat emblem of Cardiff Canton depot has just backed a rake of empty CDA wagons into the reception road at Rocks Dryers, then uncoupled from them to run out to Goonbarrow Junction on 18 April 1995. Loaded CDA wagons stand on the adjacent line, and Goonbarrow Junction signalbox is to the left. *Maurice Dart*

Right: The branch line to Carbis Wharf from Bugle was increasingly an idiosyncrasy from the operating standpoint as traffic over it became more and more erratic. The end was inevitable when the kiln which it served was scheduled for closure, and on 19 June 1989 No 37669 drifts past the woebegone station at Bugle to collect the very last wagon to pass along the branch. *Maurice Dart*

Above: During its passage along the Carbis branch on the last trip over the line, No 37669 has passed over Rosemellyn crossing. The gates are worked by the shunter who, on the warm summer's day, wearing shorts beneath his dustcoat, climbs over the gate to rejoin the loco. *Maurice Dart*

Right: No 37669 negotiates the grass-grown track to reach Great Wheal Prosper kiln at the end of the branch line to Carbis Wharf — another view of the last train to run over the branch. The stacks of the clay pan kiln and of Carbis brickworks kilns still dominate the background. St Blazey drivers had complained of 'wheel slip' on the branch, the reason for which is apparent. *Maurice Dart*

Left: On 19 June 1989 the last traffic over the Carbis Wharf branch has passed beneath the bridge east of Great Wheal Prosper kiln as No 37669 takes its solitary Tiger wagon to Goonbarrow Junction. On the top right of the photo can be seen part of West Goonbarrow pan kiln which was served by a siding off the branch. *Maurice Dart*

Right: The Burngullow to Irvine china clay slurry tank train passes through St Austell with its load of 'silver bullets' on 8 September 1991 hauled by No 37417 *Highland Region* in InterCity livery and No 37670 in grey with Railfreight Distribution decals. *Maurice Dart*

Left: No 37669 passes eastbound through St Austell on 26 August 1993 with a short load of six CDA wagons, probably from Parkandillick. The loco has the St Blazey depot lizard plate and Railfreight Distribution decals. *Maurice Dart*

Above: A new slurry plant was commissioned at Blackpool during 1989, mainly to supply Caledonian Paper Mills at Irvine. To cater for the increased output and rail traffic, together with modernised facilities for cleaning out and loading the new 'silver bullet' clay slurry tank wagons, a new and improved track layout was put in. Grant Lyon Eagre was the contractor for this scheme, and with the work progressing well on 6 March 1989 a skip wagon dwarfs the small diesel loco which is standing on newly laid track amid fresh ballast. *Maurice Dart*

*Left: Ex-BR Class 08 No 08398, by this date identified as P402D *Annabel*, required attention to its wheels, work which was to be undertaken at Laira depot's wheel lathe. It is being prepared for the journey by three ECCI engineers at Blackpool sidings on 17 August 1992. *Maurice Dart*

Above: Following the improved track layout at Blackpool, ECCI purchased another Class 08 shunter from British Rail to shunt in the sidings. The ex-BR loco No 08320 was renumbered P400D and given the name *Susan*. It is 09.15 at Blackpool sidings on 22 October 1996 and No 60033, by now renamed *Tees-Steel Express*, awaits departure with grimy slurry tank wagons with the loco in Transrail livery bound for Irvine, whilst *Susan* stands idling in front of the slurry loading area. *Maurice Dart*

Left: Following the transfer of No 08398 *Annabel* from Blackpool sidings to Rocks Dryers during periods when No 08320 *Susan* was out of service, it was necessary to bring 4wDH P403D *Denise* down around the corner from Crugwallins siding (to which location it had been transferred from Rocks Dryers) to shunt there. This was the case on 22 November 1993 when *Denise* is shunting slurry tank wagons through the washing out facility at Blackpool sidings. *Maurice Dart*

Right: Railfreight grey-liveried No 37672 *Freight Transport Association* stands alongside the shunter's cabin at Burngullow awaiting permission to proceed along the Cornwall Junction line to Drinnick. The lizard emblem plate of St Blazey depot is prominent in this view taken on 22 July 1991. *Maurice Dart*

Above: A Class 47 in Railfreight grey livery with a large BR logo brings loaded clay hood wagons bound for Fowey yard off the Cornwall Junction line at Burngullow in April 1987. The remnants of the Cornwall Railway station building are visible on the up side of the singled main line to Truro and Penzance. What was once the station approach road on the down side leads to the then extant signalbox which was soon to be replaced by a panel in Par signalbox. *John Vaughan*

Right: Crugwallins siding, which serves Burngullow Tube Press, diverges to the right less than a quarter of a mile along the branch line from Burngullow to Parkandillick. As can be seen, the layout there is very cramped and restricts the loading capacity, hence the plans to lay in a new connection from the opposite direction to serve Burngullow Road Store which also holds clay from the Tube Press. On 13 September 1995 4wDH No P403D *Denise* is running back towards the covered loading area, beneath which is standing one of the loading personnel. Afterwards the loco will run forward on to the rear end of the rake of CDA wagons and haul them through the loading area, stopping whilst pairs of wagons are loaded. *Maurice Dart*

Left: Nanpean Wharf presents a busy scene in July 1986 as grey-liveried No 37696 shunts air-braked stock in the pair of sidings which also contain empty clay hood wagons. *John Vaughan*

Above: Having at times been used for loading calcified seaweed into wagons, the one-time GWR public goods station at Drinnick Mill, alias Nanpean Wharf, now sees use as a storage area for out-of-use wagons such as these small clay slurry tanks awaiting sale for scrapping on 7 August 1996. *Maurice Dart*

Above: From just south of Nanpean Wharf a line diverges and passes below the main branch immediately north of the site of the control office at Drinnick Mill. This line opens out into three lines which descend on a gradient of 1 in 40 plus, to serve kilns, a clay mill and a bag store, all of which are now disused. It also threw off a siding which served the now-demolished coal-fired power station on which seven empty coal hopper wagons are standing on 19 April 1986. The bridge carrying the main branch is in the background. *Maurice Dart*

Right: No 37673 descends the incline on the Drinnick low-level lines, about to pass Drinnick No 5 kiln on 14 May 1992 to collect one Polybulk wagon from Drinnick No 7 kiln. This was the last rail traffic from that point. *Maurice Dart*

Left: Further along the low-level lines at Drinnick the gradient eases somewhat. No 37673 is passing this point on 14 May 1992, adjacent to Drinnick No 6 kiln, to collect the last wagon to leave Drinnick No 7 kiln. The driver keeps a look-out to monitor the progress down the incline. *Maurice Dart*

Above: Oh my! When 0-4-0DH No P401D *Sharon* was transferred from Marsh Mills, before it was sent to take up duty at Moorswater, it was taken to the Western Excavating Co's depot and workshop at Quarry Close, Nanpean (which was part of the ECCI group) to be overhauled and repainted. During this operation the loco was jacked up in the non-rail-served yard whilst its wheels were away at Doncaster Works for reprofiling; it is seen in this yard on 8 September 1989. *Maurice Dart*

Left: It is truly amazing what can sometimes be located. This bodyless internal-user four-wheeled wagon was found on 17 June 1989 lurking at the extreme end of Goonvean siding on rails which are barely visible amongst the grass and thick clay. This siding served a string of pan kilns, one of which is visible behind the truck. All of the kilns became disused, causing the siding to close to traffic during the 1970s, but this wagon survived at the very end, being used as a convenient walkway linking buildings on opposite sides of the siding. *Maurice Dart*

Right: In May 1987 a long string of loaded clay hood wagons has passed under Kernick bridge and the site where Trethosa siding veered off left. The truncated portion of Little Treviscoe siding is visible to the right of the centre part of the train, which is hauled by No 50047 *Swiftsure*. *John Vaughan*

Left: On 3 October 1985 loaded clay hood wagons are shunted at Kernick sidings by blue-liveried No 37222 which is leading Railfreight grey-liveried No 37196 *Tre Pol and Pen. John Vaughan*

Above left: Prior to the arrival of an ECCI locomotive at Treviscoe, all wagons on the siding and also at adjacent Kernick were positioned for loading using this dumper which had been modified for the purpose by fitting a large plate at each end. It was numbered P390D and is inside the covered loading area at Treviscoe on 8 September 1989. *Maurice Dart*

Above: To shunt and position wagons for loading at Treviscoe and Kernick sidings, ECCI obtained a Trackmobile 95TM diesel-mechanical rail/road locomotive, the main drive on which was to the railway wheels. Carrying its Western Excavating ECCI Ltd markings, it stands on Kernick siding on 11 September 1992, displaying its identity of No P404D *Elaine*, ready to give a visiting member of the Branch Line Society a private railtour of the sidings at this location. The member in question is conversing with the loco's driver against a backdrop of Kernick Mica Dam. *Maurice Dart*

Above: No 37174 propels some Tiger wagons into Kernick sidings which, similarly to the running line, is on a gradient of 1 in 50 at this point. The remainder of the train has been left on the branch for onward transit to Parkandillick on 19 August 1999. *Maurice Dart*

Right: No P404D *Elaine* is seen inside the loading area at Treviscoe where it is busy positioning CDA wagons for loading on 26 February 1992. It is another gloriously wet day, which made the powerful rail/road machine struggle to maintain adhesion once it moved outside the cover of the loading shed. *Maurice Dart*

Left: Immediately south of Parkandillick the line climbs at 1 in 40 to reach Treviscoe, and on 2 September 1999 No 37667 in EWS livery is descending the bank with empty CDA wagons. *Maurice Dart*

Right: On 2 September 1999 No 37667 in EWS livery is on a long line of CDA wagons at Parkandillick sidings. The front portion of the train is loaded and the rear portion empty, having been brought in by the loco from Fowey. The loco ran round the empties, collected the loaded wagons from the covered loading area which is hidden from the camera, joined the consist up and was then ready to pull forward before propelling the whole train backwards to place the empty wagons in position for loading. After splitting, the loaded wagons will be taken by the loco to Fowey. Beyond the wagons the line once continued to St Dennis Junction. *Maurice Dart*

Left: The scene at Parkandillick on 10 July 1987 as No 47148 takes a rake of loaded clay hoods out of the sidings and starts the climb up the 1 in 40 bank at the commencement of the journey to Fowey. *Maurice Dart*

Right: At the south loading bay at Parkandillick on 1 June 1994, No 37229 in the livery of the Coal Sector stands coupled to a rake of Tiger wagons with which it is about to depart to Fowey. *Maurice Dart*

Left: No 37671 *Tre Pol and Pen* with inspection saloon No DB99506 is seen at St Dennis Junction on 30 October 1991 when the entourage traversed the china clay lines around St Austell. The grass-grown remnants of St Dennis Junction yard are to the right, beyond which the route once continued to Parkandillick. The line to Par via Roche, Bugle and Luxulyan is curving away left towards Goss Moor. *Maurice Dart*

Above: No 37669 brings a train of empty CDA wagons bound for Rocks Dryers around the curve from Par past St Blazey yard on 28 April 1993. *Maurice Dart*

Left: The unique Railfreight-modified Class 50 diesel-electric, No 50149 *Defiance*, stands alongside a Class 37 on 22 April 1988 on one of the lines which radiate off the turntable at St Blazey depot. The loco carries a Laira depot shedplate depicting the *Mayflower* vessel. *Maurice Dart*

Right: The vacuum-operated 71ft turntable at St Blazey depot is seen on 26 March 1991 with No 37670 astride it, sandwiched between No 37420 in InterCity livery and No 37673. Two lines of CDA wagons stand outside the original Cornwall Minerals Railway wagon works which now houses the maintenance depot. *Maurice Dart*

Left: St Blazey depot on a sunny Sunday morning, 15 August 1993, finds No 37671 *Tre Pol and Pen* on the turntable which is being manually turned by depot engineering foreman Rod Olver whilst its crew look on, ready to reboard the loco to drive it on to one of the depot's yard roads. The turntable is maintained in working order and is used to turn '08' locos for use at Fowey, along with CDA wagons and other locos, to ease flange wear caused by negotiating sharp curves on the clay branch lines. *Maurice Dart*

Below left: The old Cornwall Minerals Railway wagon repair shop at St Blazey was modernised to carry out servicing of wagons and locomotives, in the process of which it was reduced to two roads instead of the original three to permit better clearance for machinery and gantries to be installed. InterCity-liveried No 37416 carrying the unofficial name 'Mt Fuji' stands in the yard alongside the maintenance depot in company with Nos 37669 and 37411 on 4 July 1993. *Maurice Dart*

Right: On 17 May 1995 No 37668 halts on the line from St Blazey to Par Harbour prior to reversing into the holding sidings adjacent to the turntable. The semi-roundhouse engine shed is visible behind the loco. *Maurice Dart*

Left: To publicise the launch of Transrail and demonstrate some of the services which it could provide, an exhibition including a small display of locomotives and rolling stock was held at St Blazey depot on 9 September 1994, at which one of the visiting locos was No 56044 *Cardiff Canton*, this being the second Class 56 to penetrate into the Duchy. It was positioned adjacent to the turntable and as the display was only accessible to local business representatives who had been sent invitations, it was necessary to aim the camera lens between the wires of the mesh fence which surrounds the turntable area to obtain this photo. Immediately afterwards, in true St Blazey fashion, the heavens opened, sending staff and guests scurrying for shelter. *Maurice Dart*

Above right: Still in rail-blue livery, No 08576 stands by the entrance gate to St Blazey yard on 15 April 1995. A box containing 'CF', denoting Canton depot, Cardiff, is stencilled below the cabside number. *Maurice Dart*

Right: St Blazey yard on 3 August 1996 with Railfreight grey-liveried No 08819 standing coupled to a line of empty CDA wagons. *Maurice Dart*

Index of Locations Illustrated

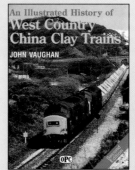 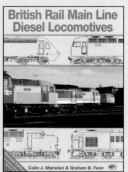